Cycles of Life

Barbara Tozer

Cycles of Life
Copyright © 2024
All Rights Reserved

To my family and friends, especially those who encouraged me in this endeavour. I hope you will enjoy the poems

Table of Contents

I Wake Tired	1
Gifts For The Teacher	2
Brighton Beach On A Fine Easter Sunday	3
Water Lily	4
Hailstorm	6
Marching Flowers	8
Forget Me Not	9
The Trains Came To A Halt	11
Junior Bake Off	12
The Day The Car Was Squished	14
This Little Sewing Basket	16
Blue Tits and Other Wildlife	17
Haiku	20
Holiday, Obsession, War	21
Dream Of Dinner At Restaurant Taste House Kimchi	25
Marigolds	28
Daffodil Tête-à-Tête	29
A Beautiful Casket	30
Bake Off	31
Stargazy Pie In The Sky	33

Dilemma	35
Camping	37
Surreal Rinse Cycle	39
Magical Transformation	41
A Private Living Space	42
Blood	44
In Sickness and In Health	45
Spring	46
The Mystery of Holy Communion	47
When We Become Ill	48
Hydroponics	49
New Diets	50
Ghastly Gum Disease	51
Imagine A Cat	53
Winter Market	55
Café Concerto	56
Two Tablecloths	57
Mobot	58
This Room	60
Art and Story Go Together	62
Bish, Bang, Bong	64
She Feels Like A Christmas Tree	65
The Engine Rolls	67

I am Watching You Play	68
It is Stir Up Sunday	69
My Old Successful Friend	70
Stretchy Man	71
Elegy	73
At The Café	75
The Owl And Pussycat	76
The Kitchen Is The Hub	78
Little Productivity On The Domestic Front	79
I Am In The Rich World	81
The Meeting	83
Beautiful Bodies	85
My Rock	87
Amazing, Amazing, Amazing	89
About the Author	91

I wake tired

I wake tired
From no good sleep. You're crying, so
I wake tired
And love you to sleep, smiling deep.
Where sleep is enabled, you rest…
No crying. You dream trauma, love.
I wake tired.

Gifts For The Teacher

Charbonnel et Walker
Premier chocolate
a reminder of the French
lessons we would deliver

The bunch of M and S flowers
A nosegay, replacing chalk dust
to inspire our delivery
of science and biology

The silk scarves,
with swirling patterns
to remind us that
there is life after school

A bright woolly hat,
for the games teacher,
who is out in all weathers,
setting a good example

Brighton Beach on A Fine Easter Sunday

After the worship sessions finish, we
watch the capable skaters on the prom.
Then, three jet bikes zoom over the shining
surf in the breaking sun. Young and old play
volleyball. It's time for another Mr
Whippy, to whip our waistlines into shape
and our stomachs into a frozen lake. Then
chorizo and chocolate sauce passes
by my eye line. I breathe in deeply, ah!
There is beach ball being taught, while the statuesque pigeons
balance on the mastheads
of the pretty sailing boats on the shore.

Water Lily

(A poem inspired by lecturer Irena George at RHS Wisley, Surrey, England)

Why do they float
these wonderful water lilies?
These night bloomers

Without the ligaium
the stems became buoyant
to withstand the currents

During the Cretaceous period
they changed from soil
to a watery habitat

The dinosaurs were around
Displaying their scary low moan
Afraid to disturb the water, perhaps

When the flower bud appears
it is scented with pineapple
and then with nectar

Pollinated by a scarab beetle who
proudly intruded and turned the
white flower pink before its death

But a thousand petals added
valuable nutrients to the food stream
The Amazon is the best place to see them

But Wisley and Kew put on a good show, too

Hailstorm

Observed during a Spring visit to Kew Gardens in 2023

The hail settled
in the hair and
in the palm house
A drum roll of hail
landed on the roof.

Several ladies rushed in
with a halo of jewels
decorating their curls.

The lake is alive, alive
with fish jumping.

A man kept his post at
the heavy iron door as
everyone came seeking
shelter for those brief
minutes.

Outside the tulips
waved, and the riotous
polyanthus applauded
until calm was restored.

Marching Flowers

Where are these flowers marching to,
in their uniforms of blue?
I think the pond is near the steps.
Perhaps their roots can feel the flow
of water that might pass below

Forget Me Not

Five hundred flowers
Five hundred days of war*
The thing that might kill us
is the absence of drinking water

How could we forget you or let you be
subject to such tyranny? You came
on airy wings to take up residence here.
A different soil but where you might thrive,
flower, and bloom, however small the room,
and despite the fear and gloom. Your pretty
faces bravely smile and make the best of every
trial.

Your children, too, grow tall and strong, learning
new ways to fit and belong while playing games
along the schoolyard wall.

* At the outbreak of war Ukrainians were able to apply to come to England for three months and were sponsored by families living in England. Local churches opened for tea and a chat. Those offering accommodation were given a small allowance to help provide necessities. Some younger people found jobs and some others returned to their own country.

The Trains Came To A Halt

It had taken a buffeting, not quite derailed,
but a wobble certainly. Along the track,
action stations. Some new plans and remedial
action.
A period of examination. Carriages eventually
put in a siding. Less activity and fewer trains ran.
The inquiry might take a while. Could it be kept
in-house?
"It will be tried, but it won't work." The station
manager …
… will need to be called.

Junior Bake Off

Was a roller coaster ride with nowhere to hide as
the icing
slid down the side

A three-tier cake, it
could produce a tear-induced drama, but it didn't
despite the constant fear

That the cake might sag
or freeze like an arctic winter, forgotten in the
freezer
for the gala teatime teaser

No one's bake
failed to impress the judges, hungry as they were
to try each one

For the sponges
they came in every flavour, Earl Gray Tea
and Popping Candy to lighten and brighten the day

Peanut brittle,
gold dust on chocolate, stewed dates, and caramel
in the mini sticky toffee puddings

Apple crumble
and cherry jam and Eton mess that was
only perfection, according to one judge

And the prize?
A crystal serving dish on which to dine
on memories of celebrity food, fun, and friendship.

The Day The Car Was Squished

The day the car was squished made us squirm.
To see the frame
damaged, the tinted windows crushed, and perfect
rectangular emeralds
scattered. Turned to trash after twenty years of
friendship and love
The tilting trailer that came to pick it up was too
small for a tall car.
But it had to fit, the driver and mad machine,
menacingly determined.
The driver was willing to help clear up but needed
a broom. I could see he
was keen to go. My grandson helped me sweep up
the scattered gems

As for the carcass? It will become a cube not alone
in death but one of
many…millions

This Little Sewing Basket

Is of its time when houses were small,
and mending was all that could make
one's clothes respectable. We still recycle bottles,
then we recycled buttons, which displeased me,
even as a child for I thought the clothes
would be more useful with the fastenings.
Once, ripped jeans were a talking point.
Now they are passe and past posing for.

Blue Tits and Other Wildlife

Part 1

Blue Tits
never stop feeding
while the fat balls
and nuts are in place

But it's sad to think
that they might not
live long, only half
the litter survives

If they don't need to
forage too far, they
become destructive
and don't behave

Who can't identify with that,
If the wine flows too freely
or the biscuit tin
is full to the brim!

Part 2

The birdcage
has two new visitors
From the wire enclosure
they try to jump
and land on the
fat balls, but usually
they miss
A beanstalk has grown up
What I wonder might climb it
looking for pie in the sky or
a fabulous egg from the fir tree?
It will be interesting.
I need a camera
to upload pictures to Spring Watch*

* A TV programme on BBC 3

Haiku

Cold and snowy day
And a half-dead tree lay low
Home to ants and moss

Holiday, Obsession, War

To me, Sidmouth is the best place in the world
for a safe family holiday,
although hazardous in the winter, not so in summer
On the horizon, my eye dreams of faraway places
Very exceptionally, someone's umbrella
was snatched by a daring youth!

This year was quite exceptionally hot,
you were unable to come to Sidmouth
Sadly, you had a hazardous infection a family member
cared for you until the sunset on the horizon
Sadly, we returned home early, daring to at dead of night
as your grandson was unwell and needed to be safe

Sidmouth had given me energy the moment I arrived
Now, I want everything at home to look daring and bright
My hotel was exceptionally attractive all New England style
safe, understated in grey and white with touches of sage green
We were able to look out to sea and the distant horizon
More hazardous now that the water quality is less good

Part 2

I have too many obsessions,
Collecting marmite jars and bean
tins that read dadz or yummz.
The joke not being lost on me
And empty tins of smoked paprika
loved by the best international chefs

Sometimes, it is the art collecting that prevents
Empty tins or bottles going to recycling
Dissaronno and punk IPA are examples of my obsessions
And extra madura pimenton de la vera, loved by all
The power of advertising often includes a joke
Which might deserve a drum roll on the cake tins

Part 3

Due to the war, grain is in short supply
If Odessa is open again and safe passage
through minefields, is possible
perhaps the threat that poorer
nations might starve will be averted
Efforts to send aid are not abating

Odessa, that big important port, that holds the grain
for mine and your families. We will not let the people starve
Though the war is not abating, the threat remains grave

Dream Of Dinner At Restaurant Taste House Kimchi

Wedded to the house
Wedded to Chef Richard
How did this happen?
She wondered this herself
f It could be an onerous task
She would perfect her Kimchi

She thought she knew how to make Kimchi
It would become the speciality of the house
She knew she was up to the task
of taking cookery lessons with Richard!
Or she could go to Korea by herself?
Somehow, she would make it happen.

She booked her flight and made it happen
Richard agreed to opening restaurant "Kimchi"
A task she needed to undertake herself
The restaurant would be called Taste House
She would entertain friends of Richard
And knew she would always be up to the task

But her staff had problems completing their task
They were unsure whether travel would happen
Strikes on bus and rail also affected Richard
He threatened the closure of Taste House Kimchi
She might have to stay at home in her house
And do all the housework herself!

But she did indeed draw up a plan herself
She would redecorate. She was up to the task
She called their abode The Happy House
And painted the rooms. She made it happen
Then, one day, she invited her friends for kimchi
And visitors came and met her husband

That night, a nightmare affected Richard
She was worried for him and herself
Burglars breaking wind-ohs to find kimchi.
Oh, what a commotion! Where was the brandy flask?
Husband feeling strange, how could it happen?
This used to be a quiet house, however
Richard and his wife enjoyed making love and kimchi
She knew herself to be happy in the house
And many a task Richard initiated and made happen.

Marigolds

Like dancing ballerinas
At the opera house
The corps de ballet
On matching points
Tutus orange and yellow
Faces hidden in ruffles
Dancing for the sun god
Glorious colours
To cheer us

Daffodil Tête-à-Tête

Yes, please, I need a date.
One or more on whom I may gaze.
We could become life partners
I will sit beside you each Spring
when you bring me as much joy as
you are able. Inspiring me with
your quiet conversation.

A Beautiful Casket

Cherry wood, perhaps, with an inscription to a daughter, a wife, a mother, a friend. Oh, that life should end too soon. How do those left behind bear it? With the help of those remaining and remembering all the good times shared.

Bake Off

He arrives at the tent. It is cold and windy.
He is allotted his space and looks around
The equipment appears very expensive, but
might the tent collapse along with the souffle?

He hopes he has time to experiment with the controls.
He knows he will be given a surprise to conjure -
a Paul Daniels on a good day, of course, he is no more,
but his spirit lives on.

He will recreate the magic he is going to knead.
Olive bread is the task, and long will it bask in his
proving oven while he sleeps on the floor, or perhaps
he will be knee-deep in dishes or have an assistant? Then

He will make a round head, an oval body, two arms and two legs.
All will be baked together. It will feed the crew, too
but only after a full examination by the lady
with the glasses and extravagant beads.

The two Pauls laughed as he knew they would
They asked if it had been fun.
"Terrifying in a good way," he said.
Then everyone laughed as the bread man ran away!*

* Bake Off is a popular TV programme on BBC

Stargazy Pie In The Sky

Stargazy pie is a Cornish delicacy
A pie where the fish peek out!

We smile at the fish,
and thank them for the feast

From our dinghy and a duvet
we gaze at the universe

And tackle the Appleoffi pie, in
a pastry case with caramel cream

and a tipple of rum to warm us
We kiss the cream from each other's

Faces and drain the rum from the cup
We paddle through gentle waves

We smile at the fish and the somnolent
moon and thank them for the feast

On shore, the fishermen are doing well
The mackerel will feed them all

As we trample up the beach,
we say goodnight and see them wave

in a haze of cigarette smoke
and the fish perfume the sky

Dilemma

She asks,
'Are we transferring from 'efficiency orientation'
to 'innovative orientation' now that we have retired?'

He replies,
'At home, the idea of a horizontal, parallel
arrangement seems obvious.
We communicate with each other and lie down at
the end of the day happy and content.'

She replies,
'But what if it goes wrong and one wants the other to change?'
She ponders her own question
'The answer, I think, is that both need to change
I think you think I've changed too much.

And on one occasion
I took the huff and left the room
Later, you appeared to have a nightmare
St George fighting a dragon?
I feel sure it was a pretence
But you won't say 'Sorry!'

So I must forgive you
A special gift I'll seek out
It might involve a change of location
I think we deserve a little vacation.

Camping

She speaks,
You are like a rambling rose
Good for fitness, I suppose
Keeps us supple
Builds our muscle
When there is the odd tussle

He speaks,
You are like a strawberry
On your bed of straw
Ripe and round
And quite refined,
With sugar

She speaks
No, no, no
It can't be that

I am quite allergic
Pay some other complement
Before I leave this tent!

He speaks,
Darling, you are all aglow
I have often told you so
Please turn over, get some rest
I am so, so blest

Surreal Rinse Cycle

Did you know
your dishwasher
has a voice?
Mine spoke yesterday

It spoke and asked me a question,
'Where would you like to visit this year?
Where would you like to visit this year?'
That was a clear sign

And it kept saying that,
and that alone!

Obviously, the dish was
talking to the spoon.
The teapot was using his spout,
and the sieve sang out

'Just look at me; I'm all filigree.'
But the teaspoons were tired.
Eventually, all was quiet.

But the fish wrapped in foil
was beautifully cooked and
craved to stay in the cool
before a final shimmer
of the shining cutlery
overcame our resistance*.

* Strange noises can give a poet an unexpected clue and inspire with a new idea. This has happened to me a couple of times.

Magical Transformation

What was the vision that I had before me?
Not sugar plums dancing before my eyes,
but a damaged leg that feels a bit dead.
Now the hip bone's replaced with a whisk and
meringues, not light as air but set like cement!
So I am not barred from mixing Gin and Tonics
My skates will come out again:
'One Fine Day'

A Private Living Space

After E.E. Cummings

Feeling blue, the maid stayed busy
in the home so spacious, but it
was still dark at 7 am.

Two cats sat beside the Aga
smiling at the thought of mice.

Faster than the latest gadget
did the good maid get to work
bustling about.

Two wine bottles that were empty
were quickly dispatched to the back.

Bins were set out very neatly,
some for glass and some for plastic
some for paper and even elastic.
Two hungry birds decided to jump
And feast on purple mahonia berries

Inside, the cleaner burst into life
as the maid danced beside
an inanimate partner.

Now the dishwasher is calling
'I need to be empty, it seems to say.'

'Yes, you do, my clever friend.'
Two clean plates are quickly removed
and many other precious things

Feeling weary, she makes some tea,
thick, strong, and sweet with sugar.

Two muscular men knock at the door,
whom she has not seen before

Men in brown with a giant parcel,
carrying ironwork for sure.
Impressive new railings for the front door*

* All in Green Went My Love Riding.

I hope my poem depicts life for those working in nursing homes in the twenty-first century. Ref, Mahonia/RHS Gardening Mahonia Oregon grape, Charity

Blood

We know it is the window to our health
It reveals if invaders
with no good intent have entered our fortress,
leading it open to attack.
Viruses and bacteria might escape detection
when things go wrong.
The body can attack itself in response.
Perhaps the medicine of man's invention
and the mystery of Holy Communion
can both help with the restoration

In Sickness and In Health

We can become ill.
Society can become sick, so
we might resolve to maintain
a healthy, trimmed-down diet
and sail away to a desert island
for a time in the jungle, but

blood has mast cells, which
reside in connective tissue
and on epithelial surfaces
initiating inflammatory responses.
We might think we can avoid disaster
but we may not be altogether successful

But why waste an opportunity
that might save the NHS money
and improve our quality of life?

Spring

I've been asleep, but now I wake
The shovelled snow to see no more
The time is set for my Spring break
I'll travel from here to another shore

Perhaps to Spain for Sun and Sangria
For more of Gaudi's gorgeous gifts
Unmatched architectural splendour
Remember, teenage love and trysts

The Mystery of Holy Communion

The mystery of communion
Is in the blood and body
Lifeblood, spilt blood, redeeming us.
Bread becoming our new body and
renewed blood, available for arteries.
Transubstantiation.
The miraculous transformation. Now, let us
be nurtured by nature's garden of Eden.
An increase in green leafy vegetables
and a rainbow of earthy things
might save our guts from busting,
might restore our blood to higher efficiency,
might become our life saver.

When We Become Ill

For none of us is forever well,
the body bands its forces together.
Neutrophils are mediators
in the fight against inflammation,
unfathomable to us, perhaps
but not to those who know

We can harm
our corporeal selves
by local factors.

Unforeseen and unprepared for
are the temptations of fast-food shops
and excessively sweet drink pops.
Dentist advises, 'Dilute them with water'
We were healthier when
we had to dig for victory

Hydroponics

Now, this digging or propagating
is sometimes carried on in tall
towers with hydroponics.

That sounds like a medical word
to do with hospital drips
fed into the arm but
sufferers with acute inflammation
can need hospital hydration.

That is one reason we all need water
it purifies the system
as prayer might.

New Diets

Stirling University say
that only plant-based food
will be served in a few years' time!

Might this have an impact on
global food policy?
And, apparently, chickens
might soon be fed on
a diet of flies, flies, flies
and it isn't lies, lies, lies!

I say, a poor life for a fly and for a chicken!
I do not know about chickens' taste buds,
but they probably need freedom
to peck worms and vegetation.
Unless the chicken has been produced in a lab,
Yes, that might be next on the menu.

Ghastly Gum Disease

The dentist recommends
Inter-brushing
Inter-brushing and flossing
stops inflammation
and might help fight dementia

Bacteria in the mouth
erode the tissue, and one's
teeth may fall out

The bloodstream
might become polluted
and may penetrate
the blood-brain barrier

Your mouth is the doorkeeper
Your dentist is your friend

So floss till you drop
until the next dance craze
follows on ...

Imagine A Cat

After Pascale Petit's Mama Amazonica

Imagine a cat
crouching on the floor
trying to open her mouth
to eat her food.

She is hungry
having been
out hunting
in her imagination!

In reality
she waits to be fed
by her owner
from a perfectly balanced can.

But for sufferers of GCA
no oxygen is available
to work the muscle
from the temporal artery.

Perhaps the vet will
offer a solution,
or a pill before
blindness sets in*

* Here the cat is a metaphor for a person with PMRGCA.

Winter Market

The season has begun; snow hasn't fallen,
but the pennies crunch, and some will go on
Christmas lunch. But are the turkeys free of flu, or
did they abscond before we knew that
Such sad happ-nings often creep upon us
when the snow falls deep. But at this market,
no birds were for sale, just specialist forms
of spirits and ale. The wind was strong tho'
not a gale, and filled with sausages, we
were not frail, so live to spend another
day fighting wars, whichever way they face
Life goes on at a pace we can't slow so
take each challenge as we go. Go, girl, go!

Café Concerto

Makes such luscious cakes
but only for ladies who know

how to balance the box on a knee
and take a dainty bite

without finding the cream morph
into an unbecoming moustache.

Cafe Concerto is not for blokes.
They are at Wembley with lads and lager.

That's how it seemed in my train-rattled dream!
Not being tempted to tidy or clean

I would have liked a picnic and some tea to
complement the concerto on radio three.

Two Tablecloths

I bought two tablecloths when the children were young
The flowery one hosted afternoon tea, boiled eggs,
and ham, not jelly and spam,
as may have been the case in my generation. But
mini meringues and chocolate eclairs, too.
A reincarnation of Lyons Corner House
remembered with fondness from a few fleeting visits.
The green one was the cover protecting the table
and where I made my daughter's wedding
cake. So slushy with sherry and brandy. It was
eaten with a spoon. Icing and marzipan glazing
down the sides. Now the cake, bar one small slice,
is just a memory. The table covered
in papers, a speeding fine, I'm ashamed to say and flats for sale.

xxxxxxx xxxxxxx

xxxxx xxxxx

xxx xxx

xx xx

x x

Mgbgt

A magical marriage, fabulous barn, hung with medieval tapestries. Friends, family, an enormous beef bourguignon toasts by the hearth. Towering wedding cakes. Symbols of a future rich in happiness. And the getaway vehicle? A ridiculous bauble of a sports car. Only it wasn't; it was superbly comfortable. Bright yellow, but could have been orange, in fashion then as now. In the middle of a recession! Maggie's closing the mines; trouble everywhere. Was this a ray of sunshine or something to provoke jealousy? A whole warehouse of baked beans could have been donated to Crisis at Christmas? What must people have thought? One teacher had her car daubed with paint. Could her coupe be next?

No, a different fate was in store. It was a sloe black winter morning. They drove towards darkest Devon for a funeral. Theirs, the only car on the road, struck black ice and somersaulted onto the verge. It was a surprise to wake upside down! No injuries, no other vehicles. Just the wind howling, a few owls hooting, and probably the Holy Spirit and a guardian angel in attendance. Police officers were notified; their car slid to a standstill. It was bad luck. Checked for broken bones, the pair were driven to the railway station, rolling stock directed towards Croydon. They travelled back in utter stunned silence. The yellow banana had tiptoed away, a write off or was it reincarnated, as they felt they had been? They wouldn't show off again in such a spectacular way. The sturdy seat belts had performed. Husband, and mother to be spared, to face joy in living and embarrassment at telling. Baby was delivered, twenty pairs of knitted bootees were presented. Those boots would soon be walking.

This Room

This room is
wrapped in bandages.
No book is read.
No drawer is opened.
She is but an interloper
using the bed and
drawing the curtains
at night.

In these Covid times
he sleeps next door.
She inhabits this room
to sleep early
and on her own.

She hasn't forgotten
the feel of you
soft and warm
or hard and muscular
or smelling of new
baked bread
or sweat and
hard work.

We are both
these things but not
at the same time
or in the same place
presently.

Art and Story Go Together

Art and story go together
One informs the other
Why would anyone bother?

When I ventured to London
Hiding behind my mask
I ended up in Trafalgar Square
And what a surprise was there

On the fourth plinth, held aloft
The giant of all ice creams
A feat indeed for the artist
Having fulfilled all her dreams

I walked a little closer
To spy a cherry on the top
But what disgusted me most
Was a fly invited by the host

By the aroma of sticky sweetness

And then, I came to see a drone
Capturing each little drop
I wondered, what did it mean?

Perhaps it was a metaphor
For the ice caps said to be melting

I don't think we are being fooled
And resources must be pooled
Global warming is in our face
Just as much as ice cream is

And we are in a race to stop
The floods
The hurricanes
The homelessness
The death

Note

Heather Phillipson's 'The End' artwork was the fourth plinth's 13th commission.
The plinth is in Trafalgar Square in London.

Bish, Bang, Bong

Bish, bang, bong, what is going on?
It sounds like artillery, a scattergun approach

I hope all the cutlery will find its rightful place
In this absurd race

To empty out the dishwasher, tick it off the list
Happy that the effort has blown away the mist…

Of dark confusion that we find
Is often clogging up our mind

She Feels Like A Christmas Tree

She is
Wearing a green dress
A band on her head. A dab of Chanel. Glasses on her nose.
Jewells on her ears and a ring on her finger.
Bracelets on her arms and
A badge on her breast. Also, spangled tights and
fluffy slippers. Then, sadly, she must,
Cover all the adornments with an overall. She is
ready to cook the Christmas dinner.
As it cooks
She goes to church
Changing her slippers
And wearing a hat
Admiring all the flowers
The choir in their robes

The organist as he plays
The pastor in the pulpit
And the congregation
In celebratory mood
She feels the joy of the festivities
And the presence of the Holy Spirit

The Engine Rolls

The engine rolls
The dustbins bang
A right royal symbol
Of community effort

Please don't strike this winter
We shall all be fitter
If we work and if we pay
An honest wage for honest work

I am Watching You Play

I am watching you play
Anthropomorphising the animals
And dressing them up in your clothes

If only you would wear some yourself
Then we could go to the park

But I am afraid of confrontation
For now, I am your slave

It is Stir Up Sunday

Good housewives getting ready for Christmas
Ready to bless the guests with something truly tasty
Certainly a celebration of international trade

Sultanas from Cyprus, cherries from Spain
Though, I need to check those packets again

Using fruit that is past its best
Will result in a pudding
That fails the test

My Old Successful Friend

Fifty million jars a year,
where could they be
filling kitchen cupboards but not all
with glee? Our DNA will help decide if we are
fan or foe, whether this dark matter is good to go
Breakfast at Tiffanies or out on the fells, sitting with a
fishing line, ringing church bells. If you're a fan, toast can
never be enough; just add a bit of butter for extra smooth
perfection. Jars are in demand because they are so pretty,
black and yellow's scary, but quite witty. Distinction
is the thing that helps a product thrive
Making all the customers feel
vital and alive.

Stretchy Man

I am being stretched too thin
When will my ordered life begin?
Feel like a plastic stretch, man
The sort
children
leave in playgrounds
When parents suddenly say,
Time to go

One day, I will delegate more
And stand at the garden gate, looking
Yet, it is nothing
to what others face
War and famine, fire and flood
Hits about the head loss of blood

Nowhere to sleep
As they step from the dinghy

Feeling sad and dizzy

We are all driven by something.
We don't live forever.

Elegy

A Faber and Faber Poetry diary from twenty sixteen, spiral bound, blue, and pristine. Purchased at the Aldeburgh festival in twenty-fifteen. A surprising event. An introduction to modern poetry and a reception where masses of ladders were affixed to the walls. A stairway to heaven, perhaps? As I read through the poems yesterday. I eventually came to October, and there I read a name, which appeared faintly; it read, 'Veronika leaves' Fifty years ago in this quaint village, families employed au pairs, who in their free time congregated at the bus stop off to enjoy London Life, including China town and a meal at Wong Kei. The postmistress taught the Cambridge Certificate, which most, but not all, the students coveted. Veronica disliked disinfecting worktops, so she came to experience my more relaxed attitude. She worked five hours of work each day. I could walk my naughty retriever in the woods, find he would slip his leash, despite puppy training and run off again as soon as we reached the garden gate! Veronika was Swiss from a farming and mountain region. I labelled items in the house, bed, bath, and bats in the belfry. On my birthday, when I went to London to take a university exam, she made me a surprise birthday cake and a pot of raspberry jam. In summer, she came on holiday with us, chasing the children into the water and pushing them along on a rubber duck. After a year, her English was good. A postcard arrived years later. Her father pushed her to church in a wheelbarrow. Her big white dress billowing out over the sides. She had married. Later they visited for tea in the garden. I nearly lost touch with Veronika, but finding the diary gave me a frisson, an aesthetic chill, because that writing referred to the time she died. Thirty years after our first meeting, she contacted me saying she and her new husband wanted a rendezvous at a restaurant near Victoria. In a glitzy cocktail bar, we enjoyed a rainbow cocktail. Veronika still retained her beautiful smile and radiant golden curls. I am fatter, but she is much thinner. We enjoyed eating Chinese food, an echo of Wong Kei. Veronika proudly told us, "The business is doing well. Updated kitchens and bathrooms are always in demand." It wasn't a long evening; we were soon back on our train home. I used the email her husband had given me; we were stricken to learn of her death but not surprised.

At the Café

The children would like something to chew on
They might have to make do with sugar cane
It might assuage hunger, but not for long
Next door, a man on his front step
is plucking and gutting a scrawny chicken
It will probably go in someone else's pot
If the person is wealthy, it might go in the freezer

For breakfast, there is porridge and
later in the day, visitors will be offered porridge
It is very good even when cold
For dinner, there will be meat and vegetables,
perhaps a fizzy drink on special occasions

Spinach is grown, but it needs water and care
It is easy to grow and popular in the city places
Goats walk along the street window shopping
and be careful to mind the traffic!

The Owl And Pussycat

Inspired by Edward Lear

Went to town in a wonderful Ford Mondeo.
They took their notes in a smart briefcase
Ready to face the new day.
They slogged away for their meagre pay
And tried to look their best each day.

"Oh, let us be married she said to him
But first my passport I must bring."
So, the very next day, they got on a coach
To the south of France,
To the land of cicadas and sun
And there at the market, he bought her a ring,
Which she put on her finger then started to sing.

The man in the market waved them away,
Happy to have earned some pay
To support his children and his wife.
Oh, happy day, oh, happy day.

Corsica is fine and wild
The crickets sing in style,
Welcoming lovers to the isle
So, they pitched their tent,
Paid the rent, and he sang on a small guitar.
Others joined in, and a dog nuzzled, too
Possibly wondering what they would do

But they couldn't possibly say…

The Kitchen Is The Hub

Or did I mean hob?
The hub is the hob in the kitchen
Surrounded, no doubt, by hubbub!

When I did my work there
It led to despair, the TV, the chatter
The noise. The air blowing in,
The air blowing out, hot and cold
From either spout.

So now I sit with the laundry.
Lovely when it is dry, not so good
When it's wet. I really must
Apportion space better, less round
The middle, more round the bust.

Little Productivity On The Domestic Front

The week is ending
Jobs are pending

My shark has been resting
A basking shark in need of a fling

My steamer, too for use on the floor
Has not managed one single tour

I've been feeding my cat, who cannot see
With the tray to his nose, he follows me

No longer does he frighten the mice
Now he is docile and very nice

I have not washed his cushion this week
The washing machine is past its peek

It will only work on a cool wash cycle
The menu now reduced to one title

Enough of this lazy life; I'll get busy
Make a timetable, not get in a tizzy.

Am In The Rich World

I am encouraged to spend money,
and I do. It is expected that I will
change my car, visit the hairdresser
regularly and possibly gel my nails.

But in my garden, I like to gather
the raspberries and the rose petals

and preserve them. I might collect
lavender to keep my clothes free from moths
or grow cornflower seeds for the birds.

My friend in Botswana
has a similar attitude; she grows beans
and dries them to sell in the local market.
She grows spinach and sells that, too.
This benefits the whole community.

The young man she employs to help
her with her work, knew all about London
He asked if I could take him there.
I couldn't steal him away from
such a friendly community, but
I hope he will realise his dream.

The Meeting

Inspired by Desert Pea by Sarah Holland Batt

I look out of the window
And see an expanse of blue

A sailing boat bobbing about
And a crew of only two

A lonely soul looking for gold
Something good to sell

But a little way off, a mum of two,
with children, I thought I knew

So down I went to say hello
'So good to see you here.'

They were happy to see me, too
The sun shone, and the breeze blew

We made a cave in which to hide
A home in which we could take pride

Soon, they had to go home for tea
It's scallops and seaweed for me

Beautiful Bodies

Inspired by Henry Moore's Sculptures

Fat, fat, fat
What are we looking at?

The elemental form
Covered in layers to keep bodies warm?

We should not worry about the shape
What we must do is gape, gape, gape

See how the beauty of the shape
might relate to our own?

However we look, we must not mock
Beauty is in the eye of the beholder

Lumps of metal, metal,
metal Shiny and warm and malleable

We want to stroke, we want to love
Put down the gauntlet, offer a glove

My Rock

You are mother and father to me
You are brother and sister, too
When I'm going non-stop
And about to flop
I can call on You for strength

If I don't, I will fail
A boat without a sail
A car with no wheels
Just think how that feels.
A case where nothing will stick

But a message to You
Both quiet and sincere
And a look at me What do I see?
Will be the antidote

I'll be free once more
To rock and roll
Find my soul
And reach my goal
Thank you, thank you Amen

Amazing, Amazing, Amazing

Not chaotic at all
Dazzling is it's construction, yes
A roundabout on top of
A motorway junction
The central raised stage
Spurs coming off
All places for strutting
For showing off the glamour
For exhibiting the
Fashion for big costumes
The fashion for smaller ones
Something for everyone, yes
Brass bands and military uniforms
A dress with bell bottoms
And balloon sleeves
(Not dissimilar from the yellow
creation worn by a soprano

Pretty Yende at the Abbey)
There was ballet, beautiful
And Shakespeare recited, too
The drone show was unexpected
A succession of birds and animals
Hovered above the stage and fragmented
The audience held aloft their phones
Their wristbands glowing red
No, it wasn't OTT it was Heart-stopping!

About the Author

Barbara belongs to the National organisation Women in Fellowship and to a Community Library where she shares her poetry and has collaborated on fundraising and contributed to two poetry collections. She also belongs to a local book club and a poetry group run by the local branch of the U3A-University of the Third Age. This organisation, which started in France, facilitates a wonderful way to make friends when work is no longer a full-time occupation. Formally a teacher, for many years now, has enjoyed singing and, more recently, has studied creative writing with the Open University.

Printed in Great Britain
by Amazon